68 Communion Meditations and Prayers

Edwin V. Hayden
Robert C. Shannon
Sam E. Stone
Kenton K. Smith

D1571758

STANDARD PUBLISHING

 Cincinnati, Ohio   3033

Library of Congress Cataloging in Publication Data

Main entry under title:

68 communion meditations and prayers

    1. Lord's Supper — Prayer-books and devotions — English. I. Hayden, Edwin V. II. Title: Sixty-eight communion meditations and prayers.
BV825.2.A16   1984   264.3   84-2
ISBN 0-87239-770-X

Except where otherwise noted, Scripture quotations are from the *King James Version* of the Bible.

Some Scripture quotations are from the *New International Version* of the Bible, copyright ©1978, the New York International Bible Society.

Foreword

Each element of worship—the singing, the prayers, the giving of our tithes and offerings, the sermon—has its special place and meaning for the worshiper. But to many of us the quiet moment when we privately commune with God during the "breaking of bread" it is the most inwardly meaningful part of the worship service.

One of the difficulties the busy minister or elder faces is the task of providing fresh and inspirational insight each week in guiding the worshiper through this meaningful part of the worship service. It is our hope that these Communion meditations will be helpful to those who are called to lead in worship at the table.

Each meditation is accompanied with a Scripture reading and prayer that reflect the theme and content of the meditation. The leader is free to incorporate as much or as little of each Sunday's meditation as he deems best.

Some of the Communion meditations are written to reflect the major sacred and secular holidays of the year. Others have been based upon hymns that are often sung during the communion service. (The hymn numbers listed are those in *Favorite Hymns of Praise.*) In this way it is hoped that the hymns we sing and the holidays we celebrate will also be used to exalt the Christ whom we encounter in the breaking of bread.

The general church membership may also find some value in obtaining their own personal copies of this book, to guide them in their private devotion around the Lord's table.

Contents

Communion
Meditations

According to Thy Gracious Word

(Hymn 432)

Scripture Reading: 1 Corinthians 11:24, 25

> For thy sweet love remembered
>   such wealth brings
> That then I scorn to change my state
>   with kings.

These lines conclude a sonnet written by William Shakespeare to a friend and benefactor. The first part of the poem spoke of disgrace and of the writer's wish to possess what others around him enjoyed. But thoughts of his friend removed all such jealous self-pity. The memory of a good friend was enough.

Remembrance can benefit both the one remembered and the one remembering. Just such two-way benefit is involved in the "gracious word" spoken by Jesus, when He broke the bread and passed the cup, saying to His disciples, "Eat . . . drink . . . in remembrance of me."

The *remembrance* word used in this connection means literally to "remember again." It was not a one-time recollection Jesus requested, but continual thought of Him. Yet it is for our sakes more than His that we must remember Jesus. He is the way of life for us, by teaching and example, and also by our being linked with Him in His death and resurrection.

When the word *remember* appears in the New Testament it usually refers to the recollection of something in Jesus' teaching: "Remember the word that I said unto you," or "His disciples remembered that he had said this unto them."

When the word speaks of remembering persons, though, it carries the idea of giving favorable attention to them and their needs: "We should remember the poor" . . . "Remember them which have the rule over you." The crucified thief requested of Jesus, "Lord, remember me when thou comest into thy kingdom."

In Communion we remember who Jesus was and what He did and said. This renews our faith and understanding. We remember Him also to renew our acceptance of His authority and to commit ourselves afresh to His will and His way. This remembrance is for our life, forever.

Prayer

Refresh our memories, O God our Father, of Jesus, Your Son. In the memorial bread may we see the body that served and sacrificed. In the cup of memories may we pledge ourselves anew to him who died that we might live. We plead in His name, amen.

Date Used: _____

Beneath the Cross
of Jesus

(Hymn 426)

Scripture Reading: Isaiah 32:1, 2

On a hot summer day in our Southwestern cities one may observe lines of people standing in remarkably straight single file on sidewalks near to bus stops. A utility pole does not offer much shade, but even its narrow shadow protects from the searing heat of the sun.

So to weary old Israel the prophet Isaiah spoke of a time when rulers would cease from being oppressive and would protect their people as a great rock in the desert offers shelter from winter wind or summer sun.

In her hymn, "Beneath the Cross of Jesus," Elizabeth Clephane describes the cross as that kind of a sheltering rock. Its shadow, she says, offers protection to the parched and weary traveler in life's wilderness.

Isaiah's promise dealt not with a rock in the wilderness, but with a king who would be *like* a sheltering rock to his people. So appropriately in her second stanza the hymn writer turns from the cross itself to the Savior whose sacrifice gives the cross its meaning. One cannot think of His death for our sins without being reminded of the guilt from which that sacrifice has set us free. We owe Him for our salvation. Grateful acceptance becomes loyal devotion. Our hymn speaks of remaining in the shelter of the cross, choosing what it offers in preference to anything the world affords.

All this and more enriches our worship at the table of the Lord. Here the burdened and weary traveler on life's way finds shelter and refreshment to renew the journey. Our problems diminish and become bearable in the light of His sacrifice. Our sin and our guilt disappear in the abundance of His grace, accepted in true repentance. Our Host at the table is more than a dying Savior; He is a living and coming Lord. Our worship is more than a lingering in His presence; it is a commitment to ongoing service in His name. The shelter of the cross extends to cover us all the way.

Prayer

We thank You for the cross, dear God our Father, because that is where Your Son gave himself for our sin. We find shelter and strength in His presence, as we accept His invitation to His memorial feast. In His name we rely on Your continued mercy and blessing. Amen.

Date Used: _____

Bread of Heaven

(Hymn 433)

Scripture Reading: John 6:54-58

It has been said that the Biblical memorials and ordinances were designed to make little children ask questions: "What does this mean?"

Jesus said that His parables were given for the same purpose. They separated the thoughtless, fault-finding hearers from the ones who really wanted to learn. The careless ones were mildly entertained and went their way. The committed followers came back and asked questions. To them Jesus said, "Blessed are your eyes, for they see: and your ears, for they hear."

One of Jesus' most puzzling parables is the one recorded in John 6:48-58, and beginning, "I am the bread of life." He said His disciples must eat His flesh and drink His blood! Shocked hearers asked, "How can this man give us his flesh to eat?"

Jesus explained briefly to the twelve, "The words that I speak unto you, they are spirit, and they are life." Those who would live in Jesus, for time and for eternity, must nourish themselves on Him. He is to be their food and drink—accepted, digested, assimilated, and made the basis for life and growth. Not only His teaching, but His person and personality, are to be their spiritual diet. So there is no real problem with the idea of Jesus' *flesh* being the *bread* of life, nor of His being the *vine,* the source of *blood,* or the *water* of life.

All this rich and varied symbolism is preserved in Joseph Conder's prayer hymn, addressing Jesus as Bread of Heaven, Vine of Heaven and Lord of life. In its words we plead that we may be nourished, healed, and built up by our daily reception and assimilation of Christ, with all He is and all He supplies.

Christ's "bread of life" parable takes on new meaning and visible form in the Communion ordinance, with His words of establishment and invitation: "This is my body . . . take, eat . . . this is my blood . . . drink ye of it."

Prayer

We come into Your presence, our Creator and Redeemer, as those who hunger and thirst after righteousness. We praise You for sending Your Son, on whose presence and person we may feast and be filled. Remembering and responding to Him, may we grow in His grace. In His name, amen.

Date Used: _____

Hallelujah,
What a Savior!

(Hymn 158)

Scripture Reading: 1 Timothy 1:15, 17

Imagine the rejoicing at the safe rescue of miners who have been trapped for many days underground and presumably lost. Where will you find another human celebration to compare with it? The height of elation at their safety matches the depth of despair at their difficulty. Heroes in the rejoicing, of course, are the rescuers who have risked their own lives to save their fellows. They now appear haggard with weariness, but jubilant in their success.

Just such rejoicing belongs to the celebration of the Lord's Supper. It reflects the feeling Paul expressed to Timothy when he called himself chief among the sinners Christ came to save, and then broke into a hymn of praise to the glorious God who had provided for his salvation. It is a celebration appropriate to all who recognize the price paid for their redemption from hopeless, boundless guilt in sin.

The same light of rejoicing against the dark clouds of one's previous despair marks Philip P. Bliss's "Hallelujah" hymn. All through its five stanzas we acknowledge the depths from which Christ has rescued us, and we recognize the cost He paid in making the rescue. Freed at last, we rejoice in Him to whom we owe it all. We who were "ruined sinners"—"guilty, vile, and helpless"—are now reclaimed because He was willing to be "Man of sorrows" . . . "bearing shame and scoffing" . . . and "lifted up to die."

This we remember in the Communion of His given body and His shed blood. The bright light of salvation shines through the darkness. He sealed our pardon with His blood, making full atonement for our sin, and now He is "in heaven exalted high." What a Savior!

When He comes, our glorious King,
All His ransomed home to bring,
Then anew this song we'll sing:
Hallelujah! What a Savior!

Prayer
Thank You, our holy and eternal God, for the boundless grace that covers our sin. In the memorial emblems of His sacrificed body and His shed blood we see the dark cost of our offenses; but in His victory over death and Hell we rejoice with joy unspeakable. Accept, we pray, our celebration of praise in the name of our wonderful Savior and Lord Jesus. Amen.

Date Used: _____

What Do We Remember?

Scripture Reading: Luke 24:36-40

An old song speaks of meeting and recognizing Jesus in glory. "I shall know my Redeemer," it says; "I shall know Him by the print of the nails in His hands."

Shall we, really? Thomas seems to have thought so. He demanded to see and feel the wounds of the crucifixion before he would believe that it was Jesus he was seeing, alive after His death. Jesus offered Thomas that means of identification.

There must, however, be some better way of knowing the Lord. Many persons were executed on Roman crosses while that means of capital punishment was in vogue. Many must have received spike wounds in their hands; and of these, some are likely to be with Jesus in Heaven.

Even if the wounds offered sufficient *identification* of Jesus, something more personal is involved in our *remembrance* of Him. His very invitation to examine His risen body came to a focus, not on His wounds, but on himself: "Behold my hands and my feet," He said, "that it is I myself." When we contemplate His sacrifice, then, should we not consider who it was who died for us, and why He died, rather than dwell on the manner of His death?

The Gospel narratives give little occasion for any ghoulish gazing at the wounds of Calvary. Instead, with a delicate simplicity the record says, "they crucified him."

Even that fact was not available to the twelve when they met with Jesus at the Passover, when He instituted the new memorial feast for them and for the church. They were asked to eat and drink in remembrance of *Him*. His death was still to come. Not until after it came would they fully understand the reference He made to His given body and His shed blood. In the Communion they would declare the Lord's death until He comes—not wounds and death as such, but the Lord's death for our sins; not death as a grim finality, but sacrifice as the prelude to eternal victory over the grave. It is the Lord whom we remember.

Prayer

How marvelous, O God, is the mercy that sent Your own Son to become a sacrifice for our sins! We are humbled as, in the memorial elements, we are reminded of His death. May we, though, see especially *Him* who died, remembering *Him* who came to be our Savior, and rejoicing in *Him* who is our living Lord. In Jesus' name, amen.

Date Used: _____

Consider the
Brow That Bled

Scripture Reading: Matthew 27:27-29

The Lord has invited His people to remember Him in the symbols of His body and blood. "He was wounded for our transgressions, he was bruised for our iniquities." Rather than tracing the wounds, however, let us consider Him who was wounded, and remember how He served with those parts of His body from which His blood was shed. Let us contemplate the brow of Jesus.

When Pilate's soldiers platted a crown of thorns and put it on His head, hailing Him in mockery as "King of the Jews," they measured their act as poorly as they measured the brow they pierced with thorns. That brow had always worn the authority of God upon it. God's Son had earned the right to perfect reign.

Earlier this night the brow of Jesus had been pressed to the ground of Gethsemane as, falling on His face, He had prayed, "Let this cup pass from me; nevertheless not as I will, but as thou wilt." Days previously, the face of Jesus had been set in steadfast purpose toward Jerusalem and the suffering that waited Him there.

From the beginning of His responsible manhood Jesus had established His course under the authority of His Father God, and more often than not He had been misunderstood and opposed because of it. Chided by His own mother at age twelve for causing worry by remaining at the temple in Jerusalem, He indicated the direction in which He had already set His face: "I must be about my Father's business."

There has come and will come, though, a marvelous changing of crowns on Jesus' brow. Revelation describes Him as the Word of God triumphant, and says, "His eyes were as a flame of fire, and on his head were many crowns."

Crown Him with many crowns,
The Lamb upon His throne.

All hail the power of Jesus' name;
Let angels prostrate fall.
Bring forth the royal diadem
And crown Him Lord of all.

Prayer

O God, preserve us from the horror of piercing our Savior's brow with something shaped like a crown, but without authority! Forgive, we pray, the lack of humble obedience with which we have sometimes called Him Lord. And purge us from the careless routine with which we have sometimes approached His table. May we honor our eternal King. In His name, amen.

Date Used: _____

Consider the
Hands That Bled

Scripture Reading: John 20:25-27

At family reunions we reminisce about our grandparents, not as they were in their last hours, but in relation to happenings that touched and molded our lives. It is somewhat different with our memories of Jesus at the Lord's table. Yet even in the symbols of His sacrifice we recall the person He was in His ministry. Consider, for example, those hands that were wounded for us.

The hands of Jesus were take-charge, sharing hands, He was the providing host at meals, breaking, blessing, and distributing bread to His guests. It was so in the miracles of feeding the multitudes, and even when He came as a guest to the home in Emmaus after the resurrection, He became the host when He "took bread, and blessed, and brake it, and gave to them."

The hands of Jesus were healing and life-giving hands. He "put forth his hand, and touched" a leper, who forthwith became clean. Friends of a deaf mute besought Jesus to "put his hand upon" the afflicted one; and Jesus "put his fingers into his ears . . . and touched his tongue" in healing him. In raising Jairus' daughter from the dead, He "took the damsel by the hand," saying, "Arise."

The hands of Jesus were active in judgment. John 2:15 tells that those hands fashioned a scourge of cords and drove out the defilers of the temple, scattering their money and overthrowing their tables. John 8:6, 8 tell that He wrote with His fingers on the ground, bringing confusion to those who would have trapped Him in the judgment of an adulteress.

The hands of Jesus were serving hands. They would be so remembered by the twelve, whose feet were washed by those hands, and who received the bread and the cup from those hands on the night in which He was betrayed.

At Calvary the hands of Jesus bled, and sealed their ministry; but now they reign and care for His own. Revelation says that "He had in his right hand seven stars. . . . The seven stars are the angels of the seven churches." All the messengers of all the churches of the Lamb of God are in good hands!

Prayer

In receiving the cup of Communion, dear God, may our hands be instructed by the hands of Jesus, to serve in His name and to His glory. Grant it for His sake, we pray. Amen.

Date Used: _____

Consider the
Side That Bled

Scripture Reading: John 19:34

"This cup," Jesus said in establishing the Communion ordinance, "is the new testament in my blood: this do ye, as oft as ye drink it, in remembrance of me." After His death on the cross, blood flowed from the spear-pierced side of Jesus—a part of His body that in life had expressed His tender affection for those He had come to save.

Let our remembrance of Jesus, then, be guided by such passages as His lament over Jerusalem: "How often would I have gathered thy children together, even as a hen gathereth her chickens under her wings, and ye would not!"

Jesus' embrace included little children. When the busy disciples would have sent the tots away, the Lord "took them up in his arms, put his hands upon them, and blessed them." Perhaps in Heaven's glory that scene will be repeated, and some inquisitive youngster on Jesus' lap will ask about the wound in his side, "Does it hurt?" If so, we may be sure of His reply: "Not any more."

Jesus' affection for personal friends was evident. At supper on the final evening "there was leaning on Jesus' bosom one of his disciples, whom Jesus loved." Jesus had "bosom friends." There was nothing exclusive, though, about Jesus' friendships. To the disciples He said, "Ye are my friends, if ye do whatsoever I command you. Henceforth I call you not servants . . . but I have called you friends."

That is a tender, affectionate friendship available to all. Its fulfillment will come as described in Revelation 7:17: "The Lamb which is in the midst of the throne shall feed them, and shall lead them unto living fountains of waters; and God shall wipe away all tears from their eyes."

Not without reason did Fanny Crosby write,

Safe in the arms of Jesus,
  Safe on His gentle breast,
There by His love o'ershaded,
  Sweetly my soul shall rest.

Prayer
Our loving God and heavenly Father, we stand amazed at the tender compassion that embraces sin-stained and rebellious children such as we. And our amazement melts into tears of gratitude as we meet in remembrance of Jesus at Your family table. We thank You in His name. Amen.

Date Used: _____

Consider the
Back That Bled

Scripture Reading: Matthew 27:24-26

Concerning the bread He offered in the last supper with His disciples, Jesus said, "Take, eat: this is my body, which is broken for you: this do in remembrance of me." Not the injury, but He who bore the injury, is central in our remembrance. Let us consider, then, the back that bore the burdens and the bruises of our redemption.

Matthew 27:26 recounts simply that Pilate "scourged Jesus" in delivering Him to be crucified. Thus was fulfilled the word of Isaiah 50:6: "I gave my back to the smiters."

The back that felt the lash was the back that bore the cross toward Calvary. Necessity at last required that Simon, a man of Cyrene, be pressed into a sacred partnership in carrying that cross.

The cross itself symbolized the heavier weight of our sins: "His own self bare our sins in his own body on the tree, that we, being dead to sins, should live unto righteousness: by whose stripes ye were healed." So wrote the apostle Peter to persecuted Christians.

Long ago the prophet Isaiah had described that sin-burden and its bearer: "Surely he hath borne our griefs, and carried our sorrows . . . He was wounded for our transgressions, he was bruised for our iniquities: the chastisement of our peace was upon him: and with his stripes we are healed ... The Lord hath laid on him the iniquity of us all."

We, however, like Simon the Cyrenian, are offered a yoke partnership with our Savior—an opportunity to join with Him in bearing our burdens. "Take my yoke upon you," he said, "and learn of me ... For my yoke is easy, and my burden is light." This we find in Communion with our Lord; and in this Communion we join also as partners and yokefellows with our brothers: "Bear ye one another's burdens, and so fulfill the law of Christ."

Prayer

We approach the table of memories, O God our heavenly Father, as those who have been relieved of an intolerable burden. How shall we ever express our thanks for Him who bore for us the guilt we could not bear? Accept, we pray, our gift of self and service in His name. Amen.

Date Used: _____

Consider the
Feet That Bled

Scripture Reading: 1 Corinthians 15:24, 25

While we live in the flesh we think of persons in terms of the bodies in which they live and move and have their being. So also we may properly think of Jesus, even as we remember Him in the Communion He established. Let us consider, then, the feet of the Savior.

Psalm 22:16 and Luke 24:39, 40 make it clear that Jesus' feet, as well as His hands, were pierced in crucifixion. But a surprising chain of thought is suggested by 1 Corinthians 12:23: "Those members of the body, which we think to be less honorable, upon these we bestow more abundant honor."

The feet become important in the giving of honor. Consider the ancient protocol of foot-washing, wherein the host washed the feet of guests he wished to honor and had a servant wash the feet of his equals, but provided only basin and water for lowlier guests to wash their own feet. Jesus noted the lack of that customary courtesy on the part of Simon the Pharisee, who had invited Him to dinner.

On the other hand, Luke 7:36-50 and John 12:1-8 tell of grateful women who anointed Jesus' feet, and He honored their extravagant devotion. One of these, Mary of Bethany, honored Jesus in another way, sitting at His feet to learn of Him. Fulsome compliments to the Master meant little, but faithful compliance to His teaching on the part of the learner at His feet meant much indeed.

Isaiah had said something long ago about the feet of God's messenger. The runner with good news would be more than welcome: "How beautiful upon the mountains are the feet of him that bringeth good tidings . . . that saith unto Zion, Thy God reigneth." How then shall we compare the approaching steps of Messiah, bringing the truth that "God so loved"?

The New Testament insistently quotes Psalm 110:1: "The Lord said unto my Lord, Sit thou at my right hand, until I make thine enemies thy footstool." And Paul adds of Christ, "He must reign, till he hath put all enemies under his feet."

Prayer

Stir our hearts and enrich our minds, dear God our Father, to know more fully the Savior whose feet bled for us at Calvary. May we sit gladly at His feet to learn of Him and to serve our eternal Lord and King. In Jesus' name, amen.

Date Used: _____

Discerning the
Present Body

Scripture Reading: 1 Corinthians 12:12-14

Amazing as it seems, the Communion at the Lord's table brings together two bodies with but a single Head! One is the body in which Jesus lived on earth, died for sinners, and arose. The other is His body, the church, through which He renders His ministry on earth until He comes again. Christ's churchly body meets on the Lord's Day to remember Him in the sacrifice He made in His physical body, and to renew her allegiance to Him as her head. Each communing member is warned that he who eats carelessly of the broken bread and drinks thoughtlessly of the memorial cup eats and drinks condemnation to himself, "not discerning the Lord's body." Is it only the physical body of Jesus that is to be recognized and remembered in the Communion emblems, or is it not perhaps also the spiritual body, His church?

Paul's warning about discerning the Lord's body is found near the end of the eleventh chapter of First Corinthians. The next chapter, the twelfth, is given to a discussion of the spiritual body, and of each member's part in it. The two were close together in the apostle's thinking.

The churchly body of Christ, like His physical

body, includes members that are very different one from another but work together, under the direction of Christ, the Head. We are not simply to endure the differences in qualities and characteristics; we are to rejoice in them. We are to rejoice also that the Communion with our Lord brings us into the company of saints in all times and all places.

All places? Assuming the same hour of Lord's Day morning worship at the table, the Communion fellowship each week would begin with the International Date Line in the Pacific Ocean and would expand from New Zealand and Australia to Asia, Africa, Europe, South America, and finally across North America from Nova Scotia to Alaska and Hawaii. Wherever the Lord has children, we have fellow members in the body we discern at His table.

Prayer

We rejoice, O God our Father, for the love that sent Your Son to save us. We rejoice in the wisdom by which He provided memorial fellowship in His body and blood. And we humbly rejoice in the privilege of being a living, working part of His body, the church. May we always honor Him in this fellowship. In Jesus' name, amen.

Date Used: _____

Always in Remembrance

Scripture Reading: 2 Peter 1:12-15

"As Uncle Dan used to say . . ."

Whatever it was your Uncle Dan used to say, it was said often enough to be remembered. It became his slogan and trademark. Now whenever you hear this saying or face this situation, you think of Uncle Dan, and when you think of Uncle Dan you hear him saying it again.

Members of the family used to smile knowingly whenever Uncle Dan would start to say it again, and someone might even interrupt and finish the saying for him. Some thought he was losing his memory in his old age, and so was becoming repetitious. Perhaps. On the other hand Uncle Dan may have been more concerned with your remembering than with his. Maybe he was willing to be thought a bit foolish if by doing so he could leave some jewel of wisdom permanently with you.

That's the way it was with the apostle Peter in his old age. He recounted again and again what Jesus said and did. He said it and he wrote it. Then he wrote it again. His readers already knew what he was telling them, but they must never be allowed to forget. Life's distractions are many and demanding; they can occupy Christians' minds and make them forgetful, or at least neglectful. Peter would not always be around to remind them of Jesus. And Peter knew the Old Testament accounts of a nation that followed God as long as some notable leader was among them, but fell away after his death. It must not be allowed to happen among Peter's friends. He would remind them again and again.

So it is with the weekly celebration at the Lord's table. It has in it the grand simplicity of the gospel, that Christ died for our sins according to the Scriptures, that He was buried, and that He rose again on the third day according to the Scriptures. There are depths yet unmeasured in that gospel, but the reminders in the Lord's invitation and His dedication of the memorial elements—the bread and the cup—are repetitious. They are purposefully repetitious, urgently repetitious, persistently repetitious, lest we forget.

Prayer

Thank You, almighty and all-wise God of Heaven and earth, that You have been so graciously mindful of our weakness and our folly. May we hear and receive Your reminders gratefully, and may we convey them to other persistently, for their sakes and ours. In Jesus' name, amen.

Date Used: _____

A Matter of
Death and Life

Scripture Reading: Romans 6:8-11

An ambulance weaves its way through traffic, siren screaming. Stop signals and speed limits yield to the emergency. It is a matter of life and death. That phrase brings a chill of desperation and dread—desperation in holding on to life, and dread that the hold will slip and death will have its final word.

How different the mood in the celebration of death and life at the Lord's table! The order is reversed. Death has been conquered and life has the final word; the delight of anticipation belongs to this feast. The reversal of order does not in any way reduce the importance of the event; it is, in fact, a key to the very understanding of the event.

The Communion, like Christian baptism, reminds us that Christ went through death to life on our behalf. He chose that course deliberately and He described it to His apostles: "I am the good shepherd: the good shepherd giveth his life for the sheep . . . I lay down my life, that I might take it again . . . I have power to lay it down, and I have power to take it again."

We must not think that the way of death was easier for Jesus because He chose it and knew it was coming. The agony of Gethsemane cries out against any such notion. That very agony underscores our debt to Him, and it magnifies the triumph of the resurrection.

Christians follow in the footsteps of Jesus, through death to life. Christian baptism is the symbolic funeral of the person each of us once was. It follows the believer's voluntary death to self and to sin, and it becomes the watery womb of birth to the new life in Christ. As said the apostle Paul, "If we be dead with him [Christ], we shall also live with him; if we suffer, we shall also reign with him."

There are death-and-life hallelujahs, then, in our proclamation at the Lord's table: "As often as ye eat this bread, and drink the cup, ye proclaim the Lord's death till he come."

Prayer

We bow in amazement, almighty God, at your mercy. Death is our portion, not Yours! And yet through Jesus You experienced death for us, in order that we might rejoice in life with You! Thank You for the Communion, in which we become acquainted with Jesus' death and life eternal. In His name, amen.

Date Used: _____

Our Host
at the Table

Scripture Reading: Psalm 23:5, 6

The Shepherd's Psalm has a place of prophecy at the Lord's table. It speaks of the good shepherd, who provides and protects, who leads and corrects his sheep. Jesus fulfilled all this and more. "I am the good shepherd," He said. "The good shepherd giveth his life for the sheep." That life-giving is at the center of our celebration in Communion.

The last two verses of the Shepherd's Psalm introduce the divine *host,* whose hospitality does not shrink from laying down his life for his guest. The descendants of Abraham were familiar with the kind of hospitality that commits every resource of the house or the tent to the protection of the guest, who may rejoice with confidence, "Thou preparest a table before me in the presence of mine enemies." One's enemies are helpless to do harm while one is under the sheltering roof of the host.

Jesus was host to the twelve at His last supper with them, and Jesus is host to every true worshiper at the Lord's Supper in the church. As host He provided and divided. He took the bread, the cup, and blessed them, and gave them to His guests. Then in fulfillment Jesus gave himself at Calvary, giving His body and shedding His blood in death that we might have life eternal.

This is the central fact in our Lord's total hospitality, but there is more. The guests come together at the host's invitation, and to reject that invitation is an affront to the host. The host's considerate attention is available to all his guests alike and equally. The responsible host directs the activities in his own house to the benefit of his guests, and none but the crassest rebel would violate the host's request. The host desires and expects that his guest will get along well together, but if in friendship among themselves they ignore the host, they affront his hospitality.

All these principles apply to our host-guest relationship at the Lord's table. The benefits of His hospitality are not available to those who depart from His presence. The wise guest concludes, "I shall dwell in the house of the Lord for ever."

Prayer

We have come at Jesus' invitation, O God, to remember Him and to accept Him as host and head of the house in which we gather. Open our hearts to receive more and more of the grace He seeks to bestow. And may we indeed dwell in the house of the Lord forever. In His name we pray, amen.

Date Used: _____

Here, O My Lord,
I See Thee Face to Face

(Hymn 436)

Scripture Reading: Revelation 22:4

Our Lord's Supper has its roots in the Jewish
Passover. To this day, when Passover is observed
in a Jewish home, there is always a vacant place at
the table. It is reserved for the prophet Elijah,
whom they suppose will come before the Messiah
as His herald. But that place is always empty. No
one ever comes.

Many of our churches have two chairs at the
Communion table, one for each person who is
praying at the table. In some churches there is a
third chair. Like the Passover chair, it is always
empty. But it is not to signify someone who is
coming. It is to stand for someone who is already
there. It is a reminder of the unseen presence of
our Lord. Christ said of this cup, "I drink it new
with you in the kingdom." Of our worship He said,
"I am in the midst."

So at Communion we communicate with the
living, ever-present Lord, the One who promised,
"Lo, I am with you always." He kept that promise.
He is here, unseen, in our very midst. We do not
just gather about a table. We gather about Him. We

do not just commune with one another. We commune with Him. We do not pray for the benefit of the audience. We pray to Him. We do not bow out of custom or habit. We bow to him. Let us remember that the attendance count is always one short. There is always one more here than we report. He is in our midst.

Prayer

O Lord, there will come a day when we will see Christ face to face in Heaven. We anticipate that day. Until then, O God, we are content to see Him here. Open our eyes to His dying. Open our minds to His rising. Open our hearts to His return. Open our lives to His presence. In Jesus' name, amen.

Date Used: _____

Jesus Paid It All

(Hymn 131)

Scripture Reading: 1 Peter 1:18,19

One community found an interesting way to boost the local blood bank. If you receive a traffic ticket there, you may either pay a fine or donate a pint of blood. If you elect to give the blood, the blood bank gives you a slip to take to the city clerk. The slip reads: "Paid with blood."

This is what happened at Calvary. Our offenses were far more serious than a traffic violation. They were capital offenses. "The soul that sinneth, it shall die!" They were worthy of death. But God forgave us; and He wrote across the record, "Paid with blood."

Only Christ's blood could have paid for our offenses. Some blood types are so rare that the people who have them are part of a network: they will go when needed and donate blood to another. Their blood is so rare it is not just taken routinely.

Jesus' blood is the rarest of all. No one else could have died for our sins. When He did die for our sins it was enough. "It is finished!" He cried from the cross. Not only did Jesus pay, and pay in blood—Jesus paid it all.

We cannot buy such blood. Though we owe our all to Him, it is a debt of gratitude we owe. We can never repay that. But we can pay the interest on it. That's what we come to Communion to do: to pledge that in the coming week we will pay the interest on that enormous debt we owe Jesus, who paid for our sins with His blood.

Prayer

Forgive our foolish pride, O Lord. Humble us in the knowledge that there are some things we cannot do, some things no human on earth can do. We thank You and praise You because Jesus did for us what we could never do for ourselves. As we lift the cup, may it remind us of the blood that paid for our forgiveness and purchased our passage to Heaven. Teach us how to show our gratitude. Teach us to give thanks in deeds as well as words and songs. Through Christ our Lord, amen.

Date Used: _____

In the Cross of Christ I Glory

(Hymn 408)

Scripture Reading: Galatians 6:14

Sir John Bowring was twice elected a member of Parliament. A brilliant man, he had learned five languages by the time he was sixteen and at his death was conversant in two hundred languages. In addition to serving in the British Parliament, he served as governor of Hong Kong. He was knighted by the queen. He wrote thirty-six books on subjects ranging from religion to politics. Nothing that he wrote is in print today except a hymn—this hymn—"In the Cross of Christ I Glory."

The circumstances for writing that hymn are significant. Sir John Bowring was sailing along the

China coast. He was passing Macao. The area had recently been devastated by an earthquake. On the shore, high on a hill, he saw the ruins of a mission church. He could tell it had been a church because the cross that had once stood atop it now stuck out from the top of the pile of ruins. Quickly he took out pen and paper and wrote: "In the cross of Christ I glory; towering o'er the wrecks of time."

What wreckage time has wrought in the world! What wreckage time has wrought in our lives! Alongside the wrecks of time we see the wrecks of sin! Then there is the added wreckage caused, not by sin, but simply by our poor judgment and our stupid blunders. In fact, if you have eyes to see, all the world seems one vast junkyard filled with the wreckage of human lives. But there is hope. Above the wrecks of time, and sin, and stupidity towers the cross! It promises that God can redeem our mistakes and heal our hurts. The Supper brings us to the cross and its restoring power.

Prayer

O Lord, we live in a broken world. And we ourselves come to You with broken hearts, hopes, and dreams; with broken lives. Turn our minds from these things to the cross. Teach us again that in the cross there is repair and restoration. As we lift the cup to drink, we pray You will raise above us the shadow of the cross and bring its power into our lives. In Jesus' name, amen.

Date Used: _____

My Jesus, I Love Thee

(Hymn 297)

Scripture Reading: John 21:15-17

It is important to tell people that we love them. Even if we are sure they know it, we must tell them. We must tell our marriage partners we love them. We must tell our children we love them. We must tell our parents we love them. We must tell God we love Him. Even though He knows all things and knows our hearts, He wants us to tell Him, to pledge our love.

We pledge allegiance to our flag. Back in the heyday of the Temperance Movement, thousands of young people publicly resolved to abstain from alcohol. It was called "taking the pledge." Here, in a far wider sense, we are "taking the pledge." Throughout Christian history, the Communion has been called a sacrament. That means to make a pledge of allegiance, to take an oath of loyalty. When we come here, we are swearing by all that is holy. We are swearing to our love. Like the framers of the Declaration of Independence, we pledge to Christ "our lives, our fortunes, and our sacred honor."

Prayer

O God, You have told us so often that You love

us. We have told You so seldom that we love You. Dear Father, even when our lives have gone wrong, we love You. Even when our lives have not seemed to show it, we love You. Give us strength so that our living this week will demonstrate to You and to the world that we do love You. We love You because You first loved us. Make this Communion truly a love feast. In Jesus' name, amen.

Date Used: _____

A Living Memorial

Scripture Reading: Hebrews 2:9, 10

Some years ago, the old Saturday Evening Post magazine carried a picture of workmen patching up one of the four faces on the Mount Rushmore Memorial. They swung precariously in a rope sling to repair the sculptures on the cliff. Though the faces of those four Presidents are carved out of solid granite, tiny cracks and fissures appear. These collect moisture and will eventually cause deterioration of that mammoth work of art. Even granite mountains decay with the passing of time. There is, however, one memorial before which time is helpless. Twenty centuries have not effaced it. It will never erode or crack or fade. Why?

Because Christ sits about the table. We commune with Him!

His memorial is not made of stone or steel. It is in the hearts of men. Nor is He a dead Christ. He is a living Lord. He himself sits with us every Sunday. His living, vibrant presence gives a timelessness to the memorial of the Supper. As long as men sin and repent, the memorial will stand tall. As long as men love and believe, the memorial will stand firm. You need not travel far to view it. It is readily available to any and to all. Its power sustains, its grace cleanses, its vitality gives life.

Prayer

Cleanse us, O God, from all our sins. We shamefully acknowledge them, knowing that our sins sent Jesus to the cross. Cleanse us. Fill us with Your Spirit. We confess the emptiness of life without You. We confess that all the things we tried failed to fill our lives. Fill us, use us, O God. If you cannot use us in some spectacular way, then use us in some simple way. Use us. May this moment of looking back toward the cross cause us also to look around. Open our eyes to the opportunities on every hand. Then lift our eyes that we may look ahead. Show us what we can be. Show us what we can do. Make our lives your instruments. As Jesus offered himself a dying sacrifice at Golgotha, today we offer ourselves to You a living sacrifice. In His name, amen.

Date Used: _____

The Work of Forgetting

Scripture Reading: Luke 22:19, 20

Here is a time for remembering; but here is also a time for forgetting. To properly worship at this table we must forget the petty, the trivial, the worldly. A thousand things that concern men are not truly important at all. We must forget our quarrels and disagreements with our fellowmen. We must forget our worldly worries; our anxieties must be laid aside. Here is a time for forgetting.

Here is a time for remembering. Here we remember the loving Christ. We remember His sinless life and we recall His sacrificial death. We remember His body, broken. We remember His blood, shed.

Here is the time and place to remember that our sins broke His heart, that we are not our own, that we are bought with a price, that the blood of Jesus cleanses us from all sin.

Perhaps we can never do one without the other. We are hindered in our remembering unless we do first the preparatory work of forgetting. So let the hymns we sing each Sunday be our time to forget and lay aside the preoccupations of the weekday world. Then, having laid them aside, we have room in our thoughts for the most important ideas that ever crossed the human mind—the love of God and the grace of Jesus.

Prayer

Forgive our preoccupation with life and its little problems. Forgive our failure to see things in true perspective. Forgive any carelessness that may lead us, even unintentionally, to irreverence in worship. Purge our minds of all that distracts. Give us clear vision of Gethsemane and Golgotha, of the upper room and the tomb and the risen, reigning Lord. We pray in His name, amen.

Date Used: _____

The Motions of Worship

Scripture Reading: 1 Corinthians 11:27-29

The world's first mechanical man was built many, many years ago in Toledo, Spain. Don Conde Alvarae had an image of himself created, and left instructions that it be placed over his tomb. It was to be placed facing the altar. It was arranged so that when Mass was said a servant could manipulate the chains and make the image stand and sit and kneel at all the proper times. It was the world's first mechanical man.

Is our worship at Communion just as mechanical? Do we just go through the motions? Do we eat and drink from habit, or custom, or duty? We must really commune with Christ here. We discern or see the Lord's body in this bread and His blood in this cup. We must repent of them and ask God to fortify us for the next time temptations strikes. To fail to do this is to put ourselves in great danger.

Worship must come from the heart. It is not just a matter of standing, or sitting, or kneeling, or eating, or drinking, or saying certain words. If we put our hearts into this Communion it can be the most spiritually helpful, spiritually strengthening time of our week. If we do not put our hearts into it, it can be the most damaging and the most dangerous!

Prayer

Forgive us, Lord, if sometimes we have just gone through the motions when we came here. Bring real emotions to our motions. Make our worship more than a mechanical exercise; make it a truly meaningful communication with You. May the somber words of Jesus, "This is my body; this is my blood," alert us to the awesome potential of Communion. Give us grace that our worship will help and not harm us. Forgive us for any care-lessness that might lead to irreverence or sacrilege. Bring before us our sins. Recreate in our minds the

scenes of Calvary where our sins were destroyed.
For Jesus' sake, amen.

Date Used: _____

The "Last Supper"

Scripture Reading: Mark 14:22-25

One of the most widely recognized works of art
in the world is Da Vinci's "Last Supper." It is not a
proper painting at all. It was not done on canvas
and put in a frame to hang in some museum or art
gallery. It was done on the wall of the dining room
in a monastery in Milan, Italy. The monks, sitting at
their supper, could look up and see this great
painting of Jesus and the disciples at the last
supper.

During World War II, bombs destroyed three
walls of the dining hall. Only one was left
standing. It was the one on which the Last Supper
is painted! Perhaps that was as much coincidence
as providence. Still, it illustrates the durability of
the Lord's Supper. Down the ages it has remained
as a great symbol of our faith and as a great
stimulus to holy living.

Not everybody agrees about the Lord's Supper.
There is disagreement among believers as to who

should preside, what container should be used, what ritual should be observed, or even who should partake. However, there is one point on which all agree. That is the way we feel when we come to the Lord's Supper. No one views Da Vinci's painting in Milan without being touched by it in some way; nor can we come about this table of sacred memory without being touched by it in some way. Believers are always touched by it in the same way. We sorrow over our sins and we rejoice in His salvation. Whether the work of art in Milan endures or not, the Supper itself will be as long-lasting as sin, as durable as our devotion, and as indestructable as inspiration.

Prayer

O God, we thank You that this Supper never grows old. The works of men fade and disappear, but Your work continues. We thank You that Your blessings are always fresh and new. We thank You that this supper is never stale. Always you break our hearts here. Always You heal our hearts here. Always You open Your great heart to us here. As just now we eat the bread and drink the cup, come into our hearts, Lord Jesus. Amen.

Date Used: _____

Come to the Feast

Scripture Reading: Matthew 26:25-29

Poets, preachers, and hymn writers all call this a feast. Since it is only bread and the fruit of the vine, why is it called a feast? Since we eat only a tiny morsel of bread and take only a tiny sip of grape juice, does it qualify as a feast?

None of us have ever wondered about that, because we know that it really is a feast—a feast for the soul. Here our spirits are fed. There is more bread here than meets the eye. Jesus, the Bread of Life, is here, and on Him our spirits feed. Here we take Jesus into our minds, into our emotions, and into our lives.

If you are physically hungry you will not be satisfied at this table. If you are spiritually hungry you will be satisfied. Our spiritual hunger and our spiritual thirst are more than filled here.

When our hunger and thirst are filled, our lives are strengthened. We develop the spiritual muscle to go back out into a dark world and live and serve in His name. Yes, it is truly a feast when we come to the Lord's Supper.

As Jesus on earth shared the poverty of our world, now in Heaven He shares with us the riches of His world. A little bit of Heaven comes to us now. It is just enough to encourage us and make us anticipate the fullness that awaits us.

Prayer

Dear Lord, we thank You for Jesus, who shares our lives so fully. We thank You that He shares our poverty, our problems, our pain. We thank You, above all else, that He died for us and rose again for us. We have nothing to offer in return, and so we offer ourselves. It is a poor gift. Receive it, O Lord. And then feed us not just on bread and wine, but on heavenly manna from Your own rich world above. Through Christ our Lord, amen.

Date Used: _____

The Lion and
the Lamb

Scripture Reading: Revelation 5:6-10

One entered the old palace of Sargon through a door guarded by colossal figures. They were winged bulls with heads like men. One entered the ancient Assyrian palace through a door flanked by huge carved lions. Coming here to worship at this table, we see neither bull nor lion, but a lamb.

In the book of Revelation, it is a Lamb that opens the book no one else can open. In the book of

Revelation, it is a Lamb that is upon the throne. Jesus is described in prophecy as the Lion of the tribe of Judah, but the Bible emphasizes His lamb-like role far more than His lion-like role.

That is what brings us about this Communion table. We remember all the lambs sacrificed by Israel down all the years. They form the background of Jesus' sacrifice and enable us to understand it. When John the Baptist introduced Him as "the Lamb of God, who takes away the sin of the world" it was understandable. His altar was Calvary. He died there for my sins, and for your sins, and for the sins of all the world.

> Dear dying Lamb thy precious blood
>   Shall never lose its power
> 'Til all the ransomed church of God
>   Be saved to sin no more.

Prayer

Dear Father, we thank You that Jesus is both Lion and Lamb. We feel secure in the knowledge that He is a Lion; we feel saved in the sacrifice of the Lamb of God. Teach us today that He still can be viewed both ways. Help us concentrate on His submissive death at the cross. Then prepare us for His victorious coming and His omnipotent reign over all the earth. Make this supper a tribute to the Lamb and to the Lion. We pray in His name, amen.

Date Used: _____

The Sign of
the Cross

Scripture Reading: Galatians 6:14

The fireman's badge is in the shape of a cross, the Maltese Cross. That is because the world's first firemen date from the Crusades. The Knights of St. John from the island of Malta had gone to the Holy Land to battle the Saracens for the possession of it. They encountered a new weapon: fire! Many knights risked their lives to save their fellow soldiers from a fiery death, and the first fire fighters were recognized. The heroism was recognized by awarding them a badge of honor— the Maltese Cross.

It is not only firemen who wear a cross. The badge of the nursing profession is a cross. Britain's highest honor is the Victoria Cross. Worldwide humanitarian efforts are coordinated by the Red Cross. Traffic safety is symbolized by a green cross.

In this subtle way, the cross touches all of life. It is well that it should. The Christ of the cross was a healer of the sick, a protector of the helpless, a Savior of the dying. There is truly no aspect of our lives that is not touched—and blessed—by the cross.

Coming here, we think much about our sins. It is right that we should. But let us not forget that

Christ and His cross also touches our lives at every point of need: health, safety, ignorance, poverty, and even at the point of death itself. No wonder we glory in the cross of Jesus Christ. It is a comprehensive cross; He is an all-encompassing Christ. Let us, like Paul, glory in the cross.

Prayer

Dear God, so many things appeal to our pride and vanity. In these moments, help us lay aside all that. We confess that we were helpless to save ourselves, that without You we would certainly be lost. We stake all our hope on Your Son and His saving blood. Our hope of forgiveness, of help in life, of Heaven hereafter—we stake it all on Christ and His blood. May the bread and the cup help us focus on the only real source of help we have, Jesus. In His name, amen.

Date Used: _____

Father, Forgive

Scripture Reading: Luke 23:33, 34

Nazi bombers destroyed England's famed Coventry Cathedral during World War II. After the war, a competition was held for a design for a new cathedral. The winning design left the ruins of the old as a forecourt through which one passed to enter the new. The blackened walls still stand, but the old cathedral is roofless and the charred timbers are plain to see. They put the charred beams of the original cross on what was left of the high altar. Behind it, they wrote two words on the wall of that devastated church. They didn't write "Death to the Nazis." They didn't write "Rule Brittania." They wrote two words that Jesus spoke on His cross: "Father, forgive!"

That's what we say when we come to Communion: *Father, forgive!* We say it for ourselves. This Supper makes us sensitive to our sins. We can no longer pretend that they do not exist. We offer no excuses or explanations. We only say, Father, forgive. As we say it for ourselves we say it also for our family. We say it for family that is here and for family that is not here. Father, forgive! We say it for our friends. We love them so much. Their sins pain us. We bring that pain here. We say it for our enemies. It is hard for us to say it for our enemies, but we do. We remember that Jesus told us to pray for our enemies and that Jesus *did* pray for His enemies. We say it for all people; Father, forgive. And having done that, we come around to the point of our beginning, and say it once more for ourselves.

Prayer

Dear Lord and Father of mankind, forgive our foolish ways. We thank you today for Jesus' prayer on the cross. The fact that He prayed for their forgiveness helps us to believe in the possibility of our forgiveness. We thank You for that Supper given so long ago. We can almost hear Jesus saying to us, "This do in remembrance of me." And when He speaks of betrayal we cry out with the twelve, "Is it I? Is it I?" O God, reassure us that our sins are forgiven, as we eat and drink in Christ's name. Amen.

Date Used: _____

City of Heaven

Scripture Reading: Luke 22:19

Lieutenant George Maduro was a member of the Dutch Resistance in the Netherlands during World War II. He was captured and sent to a concentration camp. He died at Dachau. His parents have created for him, near the Hague, a unique memorial. It is a model of a 300-year-old Dutch city. Eventually, they added windmills, a model of the Amsterdam airport, and models of other villages across Holland. Children and adults come daily and are delighted with the little doll-size city. Named Madurodam in honor of Lieutenant Maduro, it is the third most popular tourist attraction in Holland.

Christ's memorial is a table, but that table looks forward to a city. The city is called New Jerusalem, which will come down from God out of Heaven and never pass away. The Book of Revelation describes a great banquet, a wedding feast, in that city that is to come. The Bible calls it the marriage supper of the Lamb. Scripture implies that the marriage supper is only the heavenly and eternal continuation of the Lord's Supper.

Like the supper, the city honors Christ. He is the light in that city; and they need no night there. It is not a scaled-down replica of some human city, but fairer and finer than anything earth can boast. If the Lord's Supper looks backward to Christ's sacrificial death, it also looks forward to the city that is to come. Today we eat and drink for a moment; there we shall feast eternally. On this table there is only bread and wine; on that table all that delights the human spirit. About this table we gather with a few; there we will gather with all the saints of God from all lands and all ages.

Feast after feast,
    Thus comes and passes by
Yet passing points
    To the great feast above.

Prayer

O Lord, Your table is always richly spread. Whether the table for our daily bread holds much

in the hymn, "One Day." Like the Gospels, it focuses on the death, burial and resurrection of Christ.

One day they led Him up Calvary's mountain,
One day they nailed Him to die on the tree;
Suffering anguish, despised and rejected:
Bearing our sins, my Redeemer is He!

The song goes on to tell of our Savior's resurrection and ascension. The chorus reminds us of the truth we proclaim each time we come about the Lord's table:

Living, He loved me; dying, He saved me;
Buried, He carried my sins far away;
Rising, He justified freely forever:
One day He's coming—oh, glorious day!

Prayer
Even as we thank You for sending Your Son, we look forward to the day when He will return to take us home with Him. May we faithfully remember Him about the table each first day of the week, until He comes again. In Jesus' name we pray, amen.

Date Used: _____

Savior, More Than Life to Me

(Hymn 176)

Scripture Reading: Matthew 16:24-26

What is more important to you than life itself?

For some people, nothing is. They will lie, be immoral, kill—do anything—if they think they can save their life by doing it.

But the Christian is different. He has looked at life and at death. In them both, he sees Christ. As Jim Elliott said, "He is no fool who gives what he cannot keep, to gain what he cannot lose."

A Christian mother was critically injured in an automobile accident some years ago. Later she described her feelings in the intensive care unit of the hospital that first night. She said, "It was as though all of the concerns of life were placed in a great container and the most important things kept rising to the top.

"I quickly discovered that it didn't matter how much money I had in the bank, how nice a car I drove, or how fine a home I lived in. What really mattered most to me were my children, my husband, and my God. . . . And finally you get to a place where all that is important is you and God."

We will all reach that place someday. At this

Communion time we must rearrange our priorities, wherever necessary, so that we seek first Christ's kingdom and His righteousness.

Prayer

Savior, more than life to me, I am clinging, clinging close to Thee;

Let thy precious blood applied, keep me ever, ever near Thy side.

Let me love Thee more and more, till this fleeting, fleeting life is o'er;

Till my soul is lost in love, in a brighter, brighter world above.

In His name we pray, amen.

Date Used: _____

Saved by Grace

Scripture Reading: Romans 3:21-24

Occasionally we sing that verse of "Rock of Ages" that says,

Not the labors of my hands
  Can fulfill Thy law's demands;
Could my zeal no respite know,
  Could my tears forever flow,

All for sin could not atone;
Thou must save, and Thou alone.

This is what Paul meant when he taught that by doing good deeds, none of us could go to Heaven. We are saved by grace. All of us have sinned. All of us need a Savior. What we could not do for ourselves, Jesus did for us.

A man once told a preacher, "You can go to church and believe in Jesus and think you'll get to Heaven, if you want. With me, I just live by the Sermon on the Mount. That's enough for me!"

The preacher looked him in the eye and said, "Well it's *too much* for me!" And it is. None of us can honestly say we always turn the other cheek or walk the second mile. We fall short in many ways. But that's where Jesus comes in.

He died on the cross for our sins. We are justified freely by His grace. As we come about the table, let us thank God for this.

Prayer

Never let us forget, Father, that we are saved by grace through faith. We praise You for our redemption. As we partake of the loaf and the cup, may they remind us of the price that was paid so that we can go free. In Jesus' name, amen.

Date Used: _____

When the Ordinary Becomes Special

Scripture Reading: Luke 22:14-20

Common, everyday things sometimes take on special meaning. A handshake becomes signficant when it brings two enemies together as friends; a kiss is symbolic of love and commitment when a marriage ceremony is completed; a letter may become a treasure when it is the last one ever received from a loved one.

In similar fashion, Jesus took common, ordinary elements—unleavened bread and the fruit of the vine. He made them special. These elements are part of a Passover meal even today. They are easily accessible, inexpensive, and simple.

But to the Christian, the loaf and the cup will always be special. They remind us of the body and the blood of our Lord. One can imagine how thrilled the early Christians were to meet together about the table each first day of the week. This experience kept alive the memory of Jesus. It still does today.

Prayer

How we marvel at Your power and greatness, Lord. We thank You for choosing the simple and the ordinary by which to show us the profound. Let us see beyond the loaf and the cup to that which they represent—the body and blood of Christ. As we remember Him, may we rededicate our talents—simple and ordinary though they be—to doing Your will and Your work. In Your Son's name, amen.

Date Used: _____

Master, Is It I?

Scripture Reading: Mark 14:17-25

When we read the account of the last supper, it is hard for us to imagine how puzzled the disciples must have been when Jesus predicted His betrayal. They knew He had enemies—but surely not one of them! Interestingly, each of the twelve looked not at the others, but at himself. "Master, is it I?"

Helen Welshimer caught the significance of this as she wrote,

Perhaps at first they talked of little things
At supper time that evening in the spring.
The upper room was dim with candle shine
As Jesus sat with twelve, remembering.
Then quietly he said, "There is one here
Whose kiss will bring betrayal by and by."

They did not look at Judas curiously,
But each man murmured, "Master, is it I?"

Even so as we come to partake of the Communion
today, we must look inside—not at our neighbor,
not at our enemy, but at our own heart. "Let a man
examine himself," says the Word (1 Corinthians
11:23). In that spirit, may we pray.

Prayer
When there are hungry on my little street,
When I see tears or hear a heart's hurt cry
Because some one has failed to keep high faith,
May I, too, murmur, "Master, is it I?"
In Jesus' name, amen.

Date Used: _____

Peace by His Blood

Scripture Reading: Colossians 1:18-20

Everyone wants peace. Everyone. In our world
we want an absence of war; in our community we
want safety and security; in our churches, our
homes, and our jobs—everywhere we want peace.

Jesus is called the Prince of Peace, and He is. Yet
He also told His disciples, "Think not that I am

come to send peace on earth; I came not to send peace, but a sword" (Matthew 10:34). How can this be? What sort of peace did Jesus come to give?

Jesus came to make peace between God and man. Paul told the Colossians that our Lord *made peace* through His blood shed on the cross (Colossians 1:20). This does not mean we will not have conflict, that we will never get sick or never be sad. It does mean that, whatever comes, we can still have peace with God. "In me ye might have peace. In the world ye shall have tribulation: but be of good cheer; I have overcome the world" (John 16:33).

At the table we remember His victory over sin and death. These emblems remind us that we have peace with God through our Lord Jesus Christ (Romans 5:1).

As Augustine began his *Confessions* to God, he declared, "Thou madest us for thyself and our heart is restless until it repose in Thee." Christ made peace with God for us.

Prayer

We thank You, our Father, that Jesus has done for us what we could not do for ourselves. As we partake of the loaf and the cup, may they remind us of His supreme sacrifice. Grant us the peace that surpasses human understanding. May it keep us in Christ Jesus, through whom we pray. Amen.

Date Used: _____

Redeeming the Time

Scripture Reading: Ephesians 5:15-17

Time is irreplaceable. If we wasted hours this past week, we have no chance to "make them up" this week. They are lost and gone forever. Each day has its own opportunity. For this reason, Paul told the Ephesian Christians to redeem the time (Ephesians 5:16). We are to seize every opportunity, to make the most of our time.

In these moments of self-examination, perhaps all of us can think of things that we *should* have done, but didn't. For these, we must repent. We may also recall times when we did what we should not have done. These, too, call for repentance.

We must take time to be holy, to speak often with the Lord, to feed on His Word. In these quiet moments we may refocus our attention on that which is truly important. As the poet asked,

I wonder if I knew this week my last,
Would I continue living as today,
Or would I seek a higher nobler way
And would I hasten to amend the past?
O grant me grace, my Savior and my friend,
To live each day, as if it were my end.

Prayer
Help us to live with eternity's values in view.

May we seek first Your kingdom and Your righteousness. Forgive us for the time we have wasted—both in doing wrong and in doing nothing. Help us to be better stewards of our time, as well as our talent and our treasure. As we partake of the emblems today, may we resolve that we will put first things first. In Jesus name we pray, amen.

Date Used: _____

Show and Tell

Scripture Reading: 1 Peter 2:21-24

When Ulysses S. Grant was near death, reports indicate that he reflected on the difficulties of his life. His memoirs were unappreciated; his presidency was regarded as a failure; his wife was penniless. But the thing that bothered him most was that his children had not amounted to anything. Out of this deep sorrow he said, "Perhaps rather than *telling* them how to live, I should have *shown* them."

All parents know the difficulty in living before their children the life they want them to live. But Jesus was different. He not only practiced what He preached, He also preached what He practiced.

Christ's life is the perfect example. He taught us to love others, and He did it. He instructed us to serve others, and He did it. He called us to submit ourselves to God's will, and He did it. As Peter said, "Christ also suffered for us, leaving us an example, that ye should follow his steps" (1 Peter 2:21).

Prayer

We remember how Jesus taught that the greatest expression of love was for one to lay down his life for his friends. We thank You that He did that for us. As we surround this memorial table, may we recall His example. Make us doers of the Word, not hearers only. In Jesus' name, amen.

Date Used: _____

Level Ground

Scripture Reading: Romans 5:6-10

Paul told the Romans that "all have sinned" (Romans 3:23). This familiar reminder should prevent any Christian from having pride because of the salvation he now enjoys through Jesus. The ground is level at the foot of the cross. Whatever one's wealth, his status, his position in this life—

before God, he is like all other men; he needs a Savior.

When we come to the Lord's Table, we see all sorts of other people coming too. Some look like us; some don't. Some talk and act like we do; some don't. Some seem better educated and better dressed than we are; some don't. Some seem to be very religious; some don't.

We are not to measure ourselves by them. We are not to compare ourselves to them. We are not to concern ourselves about them. We are here to see Jesus.

A short time after the Battle of Waterloo, at which the Duke of Wellington defeated Napoleon, the Duke came to a Communion service. The priest recognized him. Quickly he began to ask the other worshipers to leave. But the Duke beckoned for them to stay. "Here," he said, "all men are equal."

Prayer

We never stand taller, our Father, than when we kneel in repentance at the cross. As we empty ourselves of all pride and pretense, we throw ourselves on Your mercy alone. For Jesus sake, forgive us. We come to give thanks for what He did for us on Calvary. We come to offer our lives in service to Him, and to others for Him. In Jesus' name, amen.

Date Used: _____

Never Alone

Scripture Reading: 1 Corinthians 11:23-26

After He instituted the Lord's Supper, Jesus continued to teach His disciples during the evening. He assured them, "I will not leave you comfortless: I will come to you" (John 14:18). Earlier He had said, "Where two or three are gathered together in my name, there am I in the midst of them" (Matthew 18:20).

The Christian is never alone. Like the psalmist he can say with confidence, "I will fear no evil; for thou art with me" (Psalm 23:4).

Coming about the table of remembrance each first day of the week, we are assured that Jesus is here. But He is also with us tomorrow—and the next day—and the next. At home, at work, at a party, even in a difficult situation—wherever we are, we are not alone.

A Christian preacher in Poland told visitors from America, "I have been imprisoned three times— once by Hitler, twice by the Communists—but Jesus never left me."

Prayer

We claim the promise of Your presence, our Lord, as we come about the table. We know that You are here. We thank You for the emblems that vividly picture the sacrifice of Your Son on

Calvary. We rejoice to remember His glorious resurrection. Whatever may confront us in the week ahead, grant that we may hear His words, "Lo, I am with you alway, even unto the end of the world." In His name, amen.

Date Used: _____

Identified
With Christ

Scripture Reading: Romans 6:1-7

A man once had a strange dream. He dreamed that he was present when Jesus was on trial before Pilate. He watched as the rough soldiers took Him, bound His arms, and prepared to scourge Him. Finally the man could stand it no longer. In his dream he ran and grabbed the soldier by the shoulder, turning him around. To his horror he saw that the face on the man was his own!

Jesus died for us. We helped crucify Him. Our sins put Him there. "He was wounded for *our* transgressions, he was bruised for *our* iniquities: the chastisement of *our* peace was upon him; and with his stripes *we* are healed" (Isaiah 53:5).

The apostle Paul says that we are baptized into

His death (Romans 6:3). We become identified with Him as we obey His commandments. At the Communion time, we renew our vow of allegiance to Jesus.

Prayer

Our Father, we confess our sins to You. We are sorry for them. We are sorry that Jesus had to die because of them, but we thank You for His great love. As we partake of the loaf and the cup, we ask that you will help us remember what He went through—just as though we ourselves were there. Then help us to live in a way that is more pleasing in Your sight during the week ahead, we pray in Jesus' name. Amen.

Date Used: _____

Walking With God

Scripture Reading: 1 John 1:5-7

In the Old Testament we read of those devout patriarchs who lived so close to the Lord. Of Noah it was said, "Noah was a just man and perfect in his generations, and Noah walked with God" (Genesis 6:9). What a tribute! Wouldn't it be wonderful to have as an epitaph on our tombstone, "This person walked with God"?

It should be true for every Christian. After our baptism into Christ, Paul says that we are to "walk in newness of life" (Romans 6:4). That is walking with God.

The apostle John puts it in similar words: "If we walk in the light, as he is in the light, we have fellowship with one another, and the blood of Jesus Christ his Son cleanseth us from all sin" (1 John 1:7).

As we come about the table, we do so to remember Christ's sacrifice for us—His body and His blood. For the believer, the blood of Christ is ever powerful. Even now it cleanses us—present tense—from all sin. "If we say that we have no sin, we deceive ourselves, and the truth is not in us. If we confess our sins, he is faithful and just to forgive us our sins, and to cleanse us from all unrighteousness" (1 John 1:8, 9).

Prayer

Lord, we now confess our sins to You. You know them; we know them. We are sorry for the wrongs we have done and the right we have not done. Through the saving blood of Your Son, forgive us. Grant that we may walk with You in a new life, by the light that comes from Your Son, through whom we pray. Amen.

Date Used: _____

Meditations for Special Days

What Triumph?
(Palm Sunday)

Scripture Reading: Luke 19:41, 42

Isn't it a strange triumph that leaves its hero in tears of frustration at its end? Yet that is exactly what happened with Jesus after His "triumphal entry" into Jerusalem on the first day of the week in which He died. He looked upon the city that was giving Him a hero's welcome, and He wept!

It wasn't as if something had gone wrong with His plans for the occasion. Zechariah's messianic prophecy had been fulfilled: "Rejoice greatly, O daughter of Zion; shout, O daughter of Jerusalem: behold, thy King cometh unto thee: he is just, and having salvation; lowly, and riding upon an ass, and upon a colt the foal of an ass," Jesus' own directions had led to finding and providing the colt on which He rode. Multitudes of feast-time celebrants, pilgrims from the provinces and citizens of Jerusalem, had joined in hosannas to the Son of David: "Blessed be the King that cometh in the name of the Lord!"

Jesus had accepted their praise, refusing the Pharisees' demand that He rebuke their enthusiasm. Yet with the walls of the ancient city still echoing their praise, Jesus wept over Jerusalem: "If thou hadst known . . . the things which belong unto thy peace! but now they are hid from thine eyes." The city would be destroyed because it was too busy rejoicing in its Messiah's arrival to follow its Messiah's way of life. Jerusalem had given Jesus everything except what He wanted—acceptance of Him as their Savior from coming destruction.

How do you suppose Jesus regards the celebration of the Lord's Supper in our assembly? He has not rejected our imperfect praise, but have we brought to His worship what He wants, in order that He may do for us what He longs to do? He has come to save us from sin's destruction, but He cannot do that unless we follow Him as the way of life. Remembering Him on the first day will not go far toward saving those who forget Him the rest of the week.

Prayer

O God, our Creator and Redeemer, we come praising You for the grace that sent Your Son as our Savior. Now at the table of remembrance, may we bring not words of thanksgiving only, but hearts open to understand and lives willingly submitted to the things of Christ that make for our peace. We ask in His name. Amen.

—Hayden

Date Used: _____

For One, at Least,
It Was Good
(Good Friday)

Scripture Reading: Luke 23:39-43

Strange, isn't it, that the day on which Jesus was brutally slain should be called Good Friday? For many people that day was not good at all.

It was not good for the Jewish leaders who so resented Jesus' exposure of their hypocrisy and managed His murder. But one man that day acknowledged that he himself had committed crimes worthy of death.

That day was not good for Judas, who betrayed Jesus, nor for Simon Peter, who denied Him. But one man that day spoke up boldly to confess the crucified One.

That day was not good for the scoffers—priests, soldiers, passersby—who taunted Jesus on the cross, suggesting that He entertain them with a miraculous escape. But one man that day rebuked their scoffing and declared Jesus innocent of any wrong.

That day was not good for the silent disciples who had heard Jesus' persistent teaching that He would rise from the dead, but still viewed His crucifixion as the end of everything. But one man that day spoke a firm conviction that Jesus was going to live beyond the cross and the grave.

That day was not good for Pilate, who placarded Jesus as King of the Jews, whom he had surrendered to be slain. But one man that day saw and acknowledged in Jesus a coming and reigning Lord!

He was a most unlikely hero—this executed criminal who spoke up for Jesus against his own partner in crimes and flung his own faith into the teeth of the whole mocking world. In asking humbly, this man praised bravely, "Lord, remember me when thou comest into thy kingdom." For that one crucified thief it was indeed a very good Friday.

Such courageous, glorifying faith can mark this or any other day as good for us.

Prayer
What a blessed privilege it is, dear God, to declare "the Lord's death, until He comes," by our reverent eating of the bread and drinking from the cup to which He has invited us. Enlarge our courage to speak up for Christ in the more difficult circumstances, that we, too, may hear His promise, "Thou shalt be with me." We pray in Christ. Amen.
—*Hayden*

Date Used: _____

Known in
Breaking Bread
(Resurrection Day)

Scripture Reading: Luke 24:33-35

How well do you suppose they knew Jesus—those two who walked and talked with Him on the afternoon of the resurrection day? Isn't it strange that he became known to them in the breaking of bread?

He was widely known as teacher and worker of miracles, but they did not recognize Him when He taught them the Scriptures that afternoon. Neither was there anything miraculous about the gesture with which He took bread, and blessed it, and divided it to them at Emmaus. But they knew Him in the breaking of bread, as He had broken it in feeding the multitudes, and as He had broken it in His supper with the twelve disciples a few days before.

That apparently was the way in which Jesus chose to be known—in the breaking of bread. It was a familiar gesture, belonging to the common things of life at home. And that, of course, is where Jesus chooses to live as host and head of the household with His own. Certainly it is the way

Jesus chose to be remembered in His gathered family, the church.

May we not say that the Lord's people also are known in the breaking of bread, both at home and in the church? We reveal ourselves for what we are in the three times daily gatherings with the family at the table. And if we seldom eat in company with our family that reveals something, too.

The Lord's people are certainly known in their breaking of bread with the church. How great is our love for the Lord? Well, how much does it take to keep us away from His table? How deep is our reverence for our Savior? Well, with what thoughtfulness do we come to the Communion and receive its treasures?

Though the day of resurrection is a high and holy day, it still leads us to Jesus by such familiar realities as the breaking of bread.

Prayer

Yours, O Lord, is all power and glory in the universe, and yet You have come to live with us and die for us. You have broken the bonds of death in glorious resurrection, and yet You have chosen to be known in broken bread and a shared cup at a family table. May we accept in reverent thanks, and may we respond to You in faithful service. Amen.

—*Hayden*

Date Used: _____

The Ready Receivers
(Pentecost Sunday)

Scripture Reading: Acts 2:37-42

The great day of Pentecost, seven weeks after the resurrection of Jesus, is known for a combination of grand events establishing the church of Christ on earth. According to promise the Holy Spirit came upon the apostles, enabling them to speak in languages they had not learned and to preach the gospel with a wisdom beyond their own. Peter's sermon declared the messiahship of Jesus and set forth the terms of pardon from sin. Three thousand accepted his word and were baptized, becoming thereby that body of believers who "continued steadfastly in the apostles' doctrine and fellowship, and in breaking of bread, and in prayers."

Acts 2:41 records the focal event that translated the ministry of the Holy Spirit into the reality of the church. Marvelous as the miracles and the message were, they could not have brought the church into being without the hearers' willing response: "they that gladly received his [Peter's] word were baptized."

The *Living Oracles* translation of 1826 says, "They, therefore, who received his word with readiness, were immersed." Theirs was the ready reception that one accords an expected guest. The same "receiving" term is used in Luke 8:40 of a community that welcomed Jesus because one of its citizens, previously healed by Him, had spread the word. "The people gladly received him: for they were all waiting for him."

For many years the Jewish people had been waiting for their Messiah. They had failed to recognize Jesus as the fulfillment of God's promises, but their long hope prepared the minds of many to receive the evidences offered on the Day of Pentcost. They were ready to believe Peter's declaration that "God hath made that same Jesus, whom ye have crucified, both Lord and Christ [Messiah]." They were ready to rejoice at the response given to their plea, "Men and brethren, what shall we do?" They accepted baptism into Christ eagerly as a privilege of salvation. And their continuance in the apostles' teaching and fellowship was not drudgery, but joy.

Prayer

May we, gracious God and Father, come with ready minds to receive gladly Your Word and the privilege of Your presence. Thank You for the invitation to meet with our Lord Jesus at His table. We accept it joyously in His name. Amen.

—Hayden

Date Used: _____

Standing at the Cross (Mother's Day)

Scripture Reading: John 19:25-27

It used to be a custom on Mother's Day to wear a red rose if one's mother were still alive and to wear a white rose if one's mother were dead. The same custom was observed on Father's Day. On the Lord's Day, we do not come to place a white rose on the table, but a red one. For though Christ died, he rose again and He is alive forevermore. So we do more than commemorate a dead Christ. We commune with a living Christ!

We come here to "stand by the cross," just as Jesus' mother and those other women did so long ago. In imagination, we stand by their side. We see the awful deeds. We hear the great cries from the cross. We experience the earthquake and the eclipse that attended the crucifixion. The whole purpose of the bread and the cup is to enable us to mentally "stand by the cross."

We also stand by the cross in another sense. We stand by the cross in terms of loyalty. Others may scoff at a savior who died and did nothing to save himself. They may scorn our religion and its emphasis on sacrifice and blood. But their words will not affect us. We stand by the cross.

Prayer

O Lord, we thank You that a few were faithful to Jesus to the very end. In these moments of meditation, give us courage like theirs. Give us a faith like theirs. As we eat the bread and drink from the cup, bring spiritual renewal to our lives. Give us strength to stand by Him as faithfully as He stands by us. We pray in His name, amen.

—Shannon

Date Used: _____

Reunion (Fathers Day)

Scripture Reading: Romans 8:15

Father's Day causes us to look back in memory to our past, to the home in which we grew up. Oh, the memories that cling to that old home place, and especially about the dining room table. Memories of the very special occasions; memories of the family reunions, the feasts, and the fasts; of the good times and the bad times.

In a sense, the Communion table is like the old family dining room table. We come here as a family. God is our Father. He sits at the head of the table. Christ is our elder brother. He sits at the Father's right hand. And we are all children—the children of God. Whatever we are as a church, most of all we are family. We do, in the church, all the things families do: we eat, we work, we play, we love, we worship, and sometimes we quarrel. We are family.

However, we are a big family. The Passover that preceded the establishment of the Lord's Supper was always a very intimate affair. It was observed in the home with one's immediate family. The Lord's Supper is a worldwide affair. It is open to all Christians and is observed publicly in worship. Still, it has its note of spiritual intimacy. We remember again that God is *our* Father. He is not ours only, but He *is* ours! We all must someday be separated from our earthly fathers. We never need to be separated from our heavenly Father. The Lord's Supper is our reunion with Him and with all His children. It is a time for coming home!

Prayer

Dear God, we would never have dared to call You our Father if Jesus had not taught us to call You our Father. Just now, we measure Your love for us by remembering that You allowed Jesus to die for us. We remember that on the cross He called You "Father." So we come today to remember His cross and to rejoice in Your love.

Enable us to hear again the words of Jesus on the night before His crucifixion: "Take, eat; this is my body," and "Drink ye all of it; for this is my blood."

In these moments we renew our dedication to You, our Father, and to Jesus, our Savior. We pray in His name, amen.

—Shannon

Date Used: _____

A Memorial to One (Memorial Day)

Scripture Reading: Psalm 135:13

Once a year Americans observe Memorial Day. Once a week Christians observe Memorial Day. The national Memorial Day began during the Civil War and was officially named in 1868. The Christian's Memorial Day, the Lord's Day, was set aside two thousand years ago.

At the heart of the Lord's Day is the Lord's Supper. The national observance is a memorial to many; but the Communion is a memorial to one. Alone He braved the dark battlefield of Calvary. Alone He did battle against sin, death, and Hell. Alone He won the victory.

While our national observance was begun to remember the war dead, and came to be a time to honor all who have died, it is a day of memories.

The list of those remembered grows longer with each passing year. Even if we were to keep it in its original sense, the list of America's war dead grows tragically longer and longer. And in its wider sense, including all whom we "have loved and lost a while," the list grows sadly longer and longer. But for this spiritual Memorial Day about the table it is different. We never need to add a name. We never need to honor another.

> It was alone the Saviour prayed
>   In dark Gethsemane.
> Alone He drained the bitter cup
>   And suffered there for me.

Prayer

Forgive our forgetfulness, O Lord. Every time this bread is broken, remind us of Christ's sacrifice. Then help us go beyond remembering. In our remembering, give us grateful hearts. In our gratitude, give us repentance from sin. In our repentance, give us renewed dedication to live for Him who died for us. In Jesus' name, amen.

—*Shannon*

Date Used: _____

Jesus Set Us Free (Independence Day)

Scripture Reading: Isaiah 53:12

When the Unknown Soldier was laid to rest in Arlington National Cemetery, he was given the Congressional Medal of Honor, the Croix de Guerre of France, and to these each of the Allied powers added its highest honors. He was the first non-British citizen to receive the United Kingdom's highest honor. Thus decorated, the body of the Unknown Soldier was laid to rest.

But the only honor men accorded Jesus was Pilate's crude title above the cross: "Jesus of Nazareth, King of the Jews." Though Jesus was the Captain of our salvation, though He died for our freedom from sin and death, men did not then honor Him.

God, however, gave a stirring salute. There was an earthquake and an eclipse of the sun. There was darkness at midday; and in His honor graves were opened in Jerusalem. So great was that honor that another soldier, the Roman soldier who headed the execution team, cried out, "Truly this man was the Son of God."

How poor are the honors we come to bestow on Him today! We have only to offer Him our sins, our prayers, and our love. But these are just the honors He desires. If we bring with them a renewed devotion to that cause for which He gave the "last full measure of devotion" it will be accepted.

Far worse than any political situation was our spiritual situation. But Jesus set us free! "If the Son shall make you free, ye shall be free indeed."

Prayer

You have honored us, O God, in sending Your Son to die for us and in sending Your Spirit to fill us. We do not deserve such honors. But You deserve all honor and glory and praise. As we come to Communion, we come praising You for all You have done for us, and particularly praising You for what You have done for us in Christ. His death on the cross we now remember. Cleanse our hearts. And though we can never be truly worthy, make us as worthy as we can be of such love. Through Christ our Lord, amen.

—*Shannon*

Date Used: _____

Show Me Thy Hands
(Labor Day)

Scripture Reading: John 20:24-29

A man's hands tell something about him. On this weekend when we remember the working man, it is easy to identify someone who has labored for years out of doors. Just look at his hands.

Honest, hard work is good. Paul told the Ephesians that a Christian should no longer steal "but rather let him labor, working with his hands the thing which is good, that he may have to give to him that needeth" (4:28).

The hands of Jesus also tell us something. As our Scripture from John 20 indicates, Thomas saw in Christ's hands the positive identification of Him as the Lord. As we come about the table to remember what happened to His hands, we must also look at our own. The words of B. T. Badley cause us to search our hearts.

Lord, when I am weary with toiling,
And burdensome seem Thy commands,
If my load should lead to complaining,
Lord, show me Thy hands.

Thy nail-pierced hands, Thy cross-torn hands,
My Savior, show me Thy hands.
Thy nail-pierced hands, Thy cross-torn hands,
Oh God! dare I show Thee my hands.

Prayer

As we think of the sinless hands of Christ nailed to a Roman cross, we cannot help but bow in grateful thanksgiving. We should have been there—not Him. Lord, we praise You for Your mercy and love. We thank You for Christ's eternal sacrifice that makes our salvation possible. May the loaf and the cup remind us what our redemption cost. As we look at our own hands, may we resolve to use them only in ways pleasing in Your sight. In Jesus' name, amen.

—Stone

Date Used: _____

Thanks Be Unto God
(Thanksgiving)

Scripture Reading: 2 Corinthians 9:15

At this Thanksgiving season, our minds normally turn to our many material blessings—

our food, our home, our clothes, our free land. It is appropriate that we thank God for these. James reminds us that "every good gift and every perfect gift is from above, and cometh down from the Father of lights" (James 1:17).

But there is one supreme gift for which we must never cease to praise God—His unspeakable gift! He gave us Jesus. Without Him, all of earth's pleasures and treasures would be worthless. With Him, even if we have nothing more, we are rich beyond compare.

God's gift assures us of an eternity with Him. If we trust and obey His Son, then we have nothing to fear when this life is over. No wonder we want to come about the table of remembrance faithfully. Here we recall anew His matchless love. Here we find new hope and meaning for life. Here we receive comfort and strength. Here we express our thanksgiving to God for His unspeakable gift.

Prayer

We bow in grateful praise, Lord, as we consider where we would be were it not for Jesus. We thank You for Him—for His body, sacrificed on Calvary for our sins; for His blood, His very life, given so that we might live eternally. May we never outlive our love for Him! In His name we pray, amen.

—*Stone*

Date Used: _____

Born to Die
(Christmas)

Scripture Reading: Matthew 1:20, 21

When the angel told Joseph to take Mary as his wife, he announced the coming of our Lord. "Thou shalt call his name Jesus: for he shall save his people from their sins" (Matthew 1:21).

Jesus came to bring salvation. He was born to die. The angelic host sang, "Glory to God in the highest, and on earth peace, good will toward men" (Luke 2:14). Jesus did come to bring peace—but He did it by laying down His life for our sins. Paul explains that he "Made peace through the blood of his cross" (Colossians 1:20).

It is altogether fitting that we remember His death, even as we remember His birth. The poet declared,

Though Christ a thousand times
In Bethlehem be born,
If he's not born in thee
Thy soul is still forlorn.
The cross on Golgotha
Will never save thy soul;
The cross in thine own heart
Alone can make thee whole.

Prayer

We would bow like the shepherds before the manger, our Father, as we honor Your Son. We thank You for sending Him. We thank You that He gave *His* life to save *ours*. May we give *our* lives to serve *Him*. In Jesus' name we pray, amen.

—*Stone*

Date Used: _____

A New Start (New Year's Day)

Scripture Reading: 2 Corinthians 5:17-21

When you make a mistake or mess something up, haven't you sometimes said to yourself, "I'd like to start this over again"? Most of us have.

In life, we all have wished for a second chance, another opportunity. Occasionally we will get one; more often we won't. But this is just what Jesus came to bring—a new start. He told Nicodemus, "Except a man be born again, he cannot see the kingdom of God" (John 3:3). By being born of water and the spirit, one has a new beginning. As Paul told the Corinthians, "If any man be in Christ, he is a new creature" (2 Corinthians 5:17).

As we start this new year, we have some new opportunities, some new challenges, perhaps some new responsibilities. But as Christians, we have something far better. By His death on the cross, Jesus made possible a new start in our relationship with God. We have a clean slate. All our sins are gone.

Even now as we come about His table confessing our sins to Him and acknowledging our dependence on Him, we are assured of His forgiveness. Here we find renewed strength to face the new day, the new week, the new year.

Prayer

Lord, as we begin this new year, we want to begin it with You. Stay by our side, we pray, lifting us when we fall, guiding us when we go astray. May these emblems call to our mind the blessed assurance that while we are not perfect, we are forgiven. Grant that we may be faithful unto death. Then we can live eternally in the presence of the one who said, "Behold, I make all things new." In His name we pray, amen.

—*Stone*

Date Used: _____

Meditations
for Children

The Heavenly Supper

Scripture Reading: Matthew 26:29

People have strange ideas about what they are going to do in Heaven. Some people plan on finding a fleecy cloud and taking a thousand-year nap. Others figure on trying out their wings in a little flying practice. Music lovers expect to spend time learning to play the harp.

One thing we will do in Heaven is to share together in the Lord's Supper. Jesus said so. All Christians of all ages will meet with their Savior around a heavenly table and remember, in this beautiful way, Jesus' suffering and death to bring them salvation.

If we are interested in getting ready for Heaven, this is a good way of doing it. Let's start a lifelong habit of setting aside each Sunday morning to come around the Lord's table. And then when this world is gone, we will be prepared for the greatest observance of the Lord's Supper ever held.

Prayer

Holy Father, thank You for this exciting thought of a heavenly meeting around the Lord's table. Help us to be excited now about sharing in the Lord's Supper. In Jesus' name, amen.

Date Used: _____

Jesus Loves Me

(Hymn 513)

Scripture Reading: 1 John 4:9, 10

You may feel that you have outgrown Anna B. Warner's hymn, "Jesus Loves Me." But one stanza of that hymn is appropriate for Christians of all ages:

> Jesus loves me! He who died,
> Heaven's gate to open wide;
> He will wash away my sin,
> Let His little child come in.

Jesus' love for us is the message of the Lord's Supper. We sit comfortably in this church building, but He loved us enough to bear the hurt and shame of the cross. Our Communion service is neat and orderly, as it should be, but Jesus' love led Him to endure the blood and pain of Calvary. We will go from our worship to an afternoon of relaxing or having fun, but after Jesus' sacrifice of love, His lifeless body was sealed in a dark tomb.

But this loving Savior did not remain in the tomb! He arose, and He has opened wide the gates of Heaven! And so in the Lord's Supper we remember not only how He in love suffered for us, but also how He in love conquered death.

Prayer

Our loving Father, make us more aware of this wonderful love that Jesus showed us when He died and rose again. In His name, amen.

Date Used: _____

Remember the
Upper Room

Scripture Reading: Mark 14:22-25

Imagination is wonderful. We can close our eyes and transport ourselves back into the Old West or the time when knights rode forth to rescue fair ladies. Of course, it's easier to imagine such scenes if we have just watched an exciting western movie or read about King Arthur.

Let's use our imaginations and go back two thousand years to an upper room in Jerusalem. We see Jesus eating a meal of roast lamb, unleavened bread, and other foods with His apostles. We can picture Him setting aside some bread and a cup for a special purpose.

But we have some help in imagining this. We have a table with bread and grape juice that we will soon eat and drink. This will make it easier for us to feel that, like the apostles, we are eating this supper at Jesus' request. And it will help us to remember how, only a few hours after that first Lord's Supper, Jesus Christ offered His life on the cross for our sins.

Prayer

Father, we want to remember clearly that first Lord's Supper. Help us to do so. In Jesus name, amen.

Date Used: _____

A Look Forward

Scripture Reading: 1 Corinthians 11:26

What plans do you have for the future? Are you looking forward to becoming a football star or a cheerleader? Do you see yourself as an astronaut, a doctor, a school teacher, or in some other profession?

But what happens if Jesus Christ comes back to earth before that time? What happens if this world comes to its end before our dreams come true? When we think about these things, we have difficulty in looking forward to Jesus' return.

The Bible makes it clear that if we are Jesus'

followers, the time of His return will bring joys and rewards beyond our brightest dreams. We will at last see Jesus, and we will join Peter, and Paul, and all other Christians in fellowship with our Lord. Pain, sorrow, tears and all other terrible experiences will vanish forever.

Jesus meant for us to think about His return when we observe the Lord's Supper. How thrilling it is to take the loaf and the cup and realize that soon Jesus will come for us with His marvelous blessings!

Prayer

Dear Father, we want to look forward to Jesus' coming again. Help us to realize how glorious that day will be. In His name, amen.

Date Used: _____

Two Views of the Cross

Scripture Reading: Galatians 6:14

The cross is ugly! It was a cruel instrument of execution. It brought on a lingering, painful death. Its victims suffered from loss of blood, the straining and twisting of their bodies, and exposure to the sun's rays and to insects.

The cross is beautiful! We display it in our church building, we print it on church stationery, and we even wear it as jewelry. Because Jesus died on a cross to bring us salvation from sin, it has become a beautiful symbol of love, mercy, and victory.

In our observance of the Lord's Supper we can remember both the ugliness and the beauty of the cross. It is ugly, but it reminds us that our sins are also ugly. We have disobeyed God's laws, and we have deserved eternal Hell. It took something as ugly as the cross to destroy sin's effect on us.

But when we eat the bread and drink from the cup, we should also be impressed with the beauty of the cross. Because of the cross, we have received forgiveness and gained eternal life.

Prayer

Father, we thank You for the cross and for Jesus' willingness to die there for us. Show us how ugly it is, and how beautiful it is. In Jesus' name, amen.

Date Used: _____

Saved by His Blood

Scripture Reading: 1 Peter 1:18, 19

Blood! The word may remind you of a hospital or a horror movie. You might think of a time when you cut yourself and the blood spurted from the wound. Perhaps blood is a subject you would just as soon not talk about.

But in the church you can't avoid the subject, because the Bible has a lot to say about the blood of Christ. We are "justified by his blood" (Romans 5:9). "We are redeemed with the precious blood of Christ" (1 Peter 1:18,19). "The blood of Jesus... purifies us from all sin" (1 John 1:7, NIV).

When we partake of the Lord's Supper, we must keep in mind that the bread and juice represent Jesus' body and blood. This part of our weekly worship gives us a vivid reminder of how His blood has saved us. As we look into the cup, we should be able to picture our Lord Jesus on the cross, with blood flowing from His wounds. It's not a pleasant event, but it won our salvation.

Prayer

Father, fill us with joy in realizing that Jesus loved us so much, He shed His blood for us. In His name, amen.

Date Used: _____

A Plain and
Precious Meal

Scripture Reading: 1 Corinthians 10:16, 17

What is your favorite food? Do you like steak and potatoes, or seafood, or would you just as soon order a pizza? It's nice to think about some special food, and it's one of life's greatest delights to be able to enjoy our favorite meal.

We are about to share a meal. The items on the Communion table are probably not your favorite foods. Unleavened bread seem rather plain if compared to cake or cookies. Maybe you would rather drink orange juice instead of grape juice. If the items served were the important features of this meal, it would rate as a pretty poor supper.

But Jesus himself has invited us to share this supper. The bread is not as plain as it seems, for it represents His body, broken for us on the cross. The grape juice is a very important drink, because it reminds us of how His blood was shed for our sins. Surely we shall appreciate and enjoy this supper, since it is in a special way *the Lord's* Supper.

Prayer

Our dear heavenly Father, don't let us take the Lord's Supper for granted because the emblems are plain. Help us to remember their special meaning. In Jesus' name, amen.

Date Used: _____

Are Ye Able?

(Hymn 261)

Scripture Reading: 1 Peter 2:21

The first line of this hymn quotes Jesus' question to His disciple: " 'Are ye able,' said the Master, 'to be crucified with me?' " The writer of the hymn goes on to show that Jesus asks us the same question.

Jesus was never a greater hero than when He went to the cross. During His ministry on earth He had healed the sick, cast out evil spirits, given sight to the blind, and raised the dead. But in the hours that led to His death, He bravely endured the terrible piercing of His body with nails and thorns. When we remember that He did this to overcome sin and death, we realize just how tremendous a hero He is.

This hymn suggests that we are to be heroes and heroines for Jesus. He wants us to be as brave as He was, as ready to sacrifice for others as He was, and as determined to obey God's will as He was. What better time than at the Lord's Supper to say to Him, "Lord, we are able. Our spirits are Thine"?

Prayer

Heavenly Father, help us, through Jesus' wonderful example, to become heroes of the faith. In His name, amen.

Date Used: _____

Attitude Check

Scripture Reading: Philippians 2:1-4

Imagine this: An American spaceship is approaching the planet Mars. Two of the astronauts enter the Martian module that will take them down to the planet's surface—the first manned landing on Mars.

As they get into the module, Astronaut Jones mutters to himself, "I'll go on the mission with Astronaut Smith, but I refuse to speak to him. He hurt my feelings ten million miles ago."

Astronaut Brown, who has to stay with the orbiting mother ship, is upset, too. "Why do they get the glamorous job, while I have to stay up here?" he complains. "I have half a mind to go back home to earth."

Attitudes like these would destroy our space program. But the church won't be able to fulfil its mission on earth, either, if Christians let pride, jealousy, and selfishness keep us from working together. When we meet around the Lord's table, it's an excellent time for us to let go of any bad feelings we may have toward another Christian. Let's pray that the Lord will fill us with love and compassion toward one another.

Prayer

Dear Father, make us realize how much we need one another and how important it is for us to work together for Christ. In His name, amen.

Date Used: _____

A Supper for the Steadfast

Scripture Reading: Acts 2:42

Have you ever thought about that crowd of three thousand people who were baptized on the day of Pentecost? A crowd that big must have included many young people. Imagine! Jairus' daughter, whom Jesus had raised from the dead, might have been present. Remember the young boy whose lunch Jesus used to feed more than five thousand? He could have been there. It's even possible that some of the little children whose mothers had brought them to Jesus were baptized that day.

However many young people were baptized, they "continued steadfastly" in observing the Lord's Supper. Like the adults they used this special way to remember how Jesus died for their sins. Every Sunday they ate the bread and drank the grape juice as a vivid reminder of the way in which His body was beaten and bruised and His blood was shed.

Have you made up your mind to be steadfast? Are you determined to be here each Sunday when the Lord's Supper is served? Just because you are young it is no excuse for missing this special time.

Prayer

Gracious God, keep us from using excuses that would take us away from the Lord's Supper. Remind us to continue steadfastly in meeting this way with Jesus. In His name, amen.

Date Used: _____

He's the Lamb!

Scripture Reading: John 1:29

John the Baptist called Jesus "The Lamb of God." Why did he say that? Perhaps it would be fitting to say Jesus was "innocent as a lamb" or "gentle as a lamb." But the name doesn't seem to fit Him after that point.

The key to this problem is the Jewish feast of the Passover, which began in Moses' time. Its main feature was the Passover lamb, which was to be perfect and unblemished. Such a lamb was to be sacrificed and eaten in every household. During the original Passover, the nation of Israel was released from years of slavery in Egypt. The feast was celebrated every year after that to remind the people of the way God delivered them.

Jesus is the lamb of God who was sacrificed to deliver us from slavery to sin. When we observe the Lord's Supper, we recall that though He was sinless and perfect, He suffered a terrible death on the cross. In this way He freed us from sin's power.

Prayer

Heavenly Father, guide us in understanding the rich meaning of Jesus' title, "the Lamb of God." We thank You for His sacrifice. In His name, amen.

Date Used: _____

The Greatest Event
in History

Scripture Reading: Galatians 4:4, 5

What is the most important event in history? Some people might say Gutenberg's invention of movable type, or Columbus's discovery of America, or Neil Armstrong's walk on the moon.

But we Christians know that these events are far less important than the ones we are remembering today: the death and resurrection of Jesus Christ.

If Gutenberg was so important, why don't we celebrate "Gutenberg Day" once a year? We do celebrate Columbus Day, but even on that day not many people think seriously about Christopher Columbus. Several other persons walked on the moon after Neil Armstrong did, so his deed does not seem very unusual anymore.

But one day each week, vast numbers of Christians throughout the world pause at the Lord's table to remember Jesus' deeds. They know that what Jesus did had never been done before and never will be done again. He alone died for the sins of the world and rose again.

Prayer
Father, help us to understand how special and powerful are the events of Jesus' death and

resurrection. Guide us so that we can show our friends and neighbors how important these events are. In Jesus' name, amen.

Date Used: _____

A Standing Appointment

Scripture Reading: Luke 22:19, 20

Your parents may carry a pocket calendar on which they write down all their appointments. Maybe you even carry such a calendar—after all, with church and school activities, things to do at home, ball games, music practice, and so on, you might have a very busy schedule.

Any Christian who keeps a record of his appointments should write these words down for every Sunday: "Meet with the Lord around His table." Jesus made a regular appointment with all His followers when He said, "Do this in remembrance of me." Every Sunday at the Lord's Supper, He expects us to be present.

Would you carelessly miss a ball game in which your team needed you? Would you stay home from a party after someone had given you a special invitation? If you are careful to keep appointments like these, how much more important is it to keep this standing appointment with Jesus?

Prayer

Our Father, as our appointments increase and our lives become busier, keep us from forgetting that most important appointment around the Lord's table. In Jesus' name, amen.

Date Used: _____

Table Manners

Scripture Reading: 1 Corinthians 11:28

"Wash your hands!"

"Don't take such big bites!"

"Remember to say 'Please' and 'May I be excused?' and 'Thank you.' "

These are familiar commands, aren't they? As far back as we can remember our mothers have been trying to get us to mind our table manners. And while we complain about it sometimes, we realize that without such manners we might start to look like the animals at the zoo at feeding time.

Have you ever thought about your "table manners" at the Lord's table? We are the guests, while Jesus is the host, and we do not want to offend Him. A reverent mood is one way that we can show our respect to Him. Whispering, giggling, and passing notes are very bad manners at the Lord's table, and they may also distract other guests there.

We are to think reverently about the body and the blood of our Savior as the bread and juice are passed to us. We should not take these emblems until we have searched our hearts, confessed our sins, and asked the Lord for forgiveness.

Prayer

Father, help us to please You and Jesus Your Son, with our behavior at the Lord's table. In His name, amen.

Date Used: _____

Living for Jesus

(Hymn 259)

Scripture Reading: Revelation 2:10

Do you know who Tonto is?

If you answered that he is the Lone Ranger's helper, you were right. Many years ago when the

116

Lone Ranger's adventures were on radio, the announcer spoke of "his faithful Indian companion Tonto."

We don't hear the word "faithful" used very often today. In families, in friendships, in business, and even in the church, people don't seem concerned about being faithful to their duties or their words.

But Jesus wants us to be faithful to Him. He is our Savior and Lord, and He expects us to live and serve Him faithfully, according to His will. The Lord's Supper is a special time in which we think about Jesus and promise to follow Him faithfully. As we partake of these emblems, let's remember our hymn for today and make this prayer our own:

O Jesus, Lord and Savior,
    I give myself to Thee,
For Thou, in Thy atonement,
    didst give Thyself for me;
I own no other Master,
    my heart shall be Thy throne,
My life I give, henceforth to live,
    O Christ, for thee alone.

Prayer

Our heavenly Father, help us not to be unfaithful like many people in the world, and to practice faithful living for You and Your Son. In His name, amen.

Date Used: _____

or little, this table never fails to satisfy. We thank You that the crust of bread and the sip of wine have become vehicles of spiritual food beyond describing. Feed our souls, O God. Feed them with Your Word. Feed them with Your Spirit. Feed them with heavenly manna. Be yourself, O Christ, the Bread of Life. Make this simple meal a feast—and a foretaste of the feast that is to come. In Jesus' name, amen.

Date Used: _____

There Is a Fountain

(Hymn 141)

Scripture Reading: Hebrews 9:11-14

Blood means life. The Old Testament Law explained, "The life of the flesh is in the blood" (Leviticus 17:11).

For this reason God chose to require blood offerings from His children throughout the patriarchal and Mosaic dispensations. When sin occurred, a blood sacrifice was required for the sinner's forgiveness.

The Hebrew writer tells us that this divine principle holds true for Christians as well.

"Without shedding of blood is no remission" (Hebrews 9:22). But we need offer no animal sacrifice. We need not seek a temple in Jerusalem. We need not expect a reenactment of Calvary week after week.

Christ suffered once for our sins (1 Peter 3:18). He gave His blood—His *life*—for us. Now we can sing with William Cowper,

There is a fountain filled with blood
Drawn from Immanuel's veins;
And sinners, plunged beneath that flood,
Lose all their guilty stains.

Prayer

Father, it overwhelms us to think that Jesus loved us so much that He would die for us. He laid down His life; He shed His blood—all for us! We thank You for the assurance that His blood "shall never lose its power, till all the ransomed Church of God be saved to sin no more." In Jesus' name, amen.

Date Used: _____

"This Do in Remembrance of Me"

(Hymn 439)

Scripture Reading: 1 Corinthians 11:23-26

Some of our hymns are based directly on Scripture. This is true of Helen E. Fromm's Communion song, "This Do in Remembrance of Me." After setting the scene in the upper room, she writes,

> Then take of the bread to remember
> That His body was broken for you;
> And drink of the cup to remember
> His blood that was shed for you too.

Lee Carter Maynard has pointed out that when we eat the bread we bow our heads, looking down. But when we drink the cup, we lift our eyes upward. This reminds us of the disciples as they first looked down in despair when Jesus died, but later looked up in hope after His resurrection.

> The Savior now liveth in glory,
> Triumphant o'er death and o'er sin;
> Until He shall come for His dear ones,
> Do this in remembrance of Him.

Prayer

As we assemble about the table, Father, we come at the invitation of Jesus. Bless these emblems that remind us of His death, burial, and resurrection. We commune in hope. We treasure His assurance that "as often as ye eat this bread, and drink this cup, ye do show the Lord's death till he come." Even so, come, Lord Jesus. Amen.

Date Used: _____

One Day!

(Hymn 377)

Scripture Reading: John 3:16, 17

A small boy and his father were driving past a cemetery. Pointing to the grave markers, the boy asked, "Where's the one of those things that sticks up where God was?"

"Do you mean where Jesus was?" his dad asked. "There isn't one. He died in another country many miles from here—but we don't even know exactly where His grave was. The important thing is that it's empty."

J. Wilbur Chapman outlined the life of our Lord